Let's Go
TO A DAIRY

The author and artist wish to thank Mr. J. P. Garrahy and Miss Rachael Reed of The Borden Company for their help in compiling the book and checking the manuscript.

Let's Go

TO A DAIRY

Written by J. M. GOODSPEED
Illustrated by Raymond Abel

**G. P. Putnam's Sons
New York**

G. P. Putnam's Sons   **New York**

Text © 1957 by J. M. Goodspeed   Illustrations © 1957 by Raymond Abel

Library of Congress Catalog Card Number: 57:9398   Manufactured in the United States of America

Seventh Impression

When you go through your local dairy you'll see many men, many machines and much activity. These men and busy machines are working to bring you the glass of milk on your breakfast table.

But the journey of your glass of milk really begins on the farm. So first let's take a look at a dairy farm.

Twice a day the barn on a dairy farm is a very busy place. In the early hours of the morning, probably while you're still fast

380

asleep, the farmer milks his cows. Then again in the late afternoon, after school is out but before your dinnertime, the cows are milked once more.

The dairy barn is the long big building that you see. It smells of cows, warm milk and hay. It must be kept clean, well aired and lighted. You can walk down the aisle in the center of the barn. On each side of the aisle you will see many stalls. The stalls are booths separated by iron bars. Each cow knows her own stall and will walk right into it.

At the head of each stall is the manger which is sometimes called the feed bunk. The mangers look like big window flower boxes and they hold the cows' food. Cows eat roughage such as grass and hay. They also eat grain. You may see a bucket of water or perhaps a mechanical drinking cup at the head of each stall too. When the cow puts her head down into the mechanical drinking cup, the cup automatically fills with water.

The space that you see between the head of the stalls and the side of the barn is called the alleyway. The farmer walks down the alleyway to fill the feed bunks, and the water buckets if there are no mechanical drinking cups.

Each cow has a name and number. The name and number is stamped onto a small piece of metal that is attached by a chain to the cow's horns. This name tag is called a horn button and it hangs right in the middle of the cow's forehead.

The cows have names and numbers so that the farmer can keep track of how much milk each cow gives. The amount of grain a cow is given to eat depends on how much milk she gives. This record of milk also helps the farmer to check on the health of his cows.

In the spring, summer and fall the cows go to the barn only for eating and milking. They spend the rest of the time at pasture. In the cold winter months the cows are in the barn most of the time. They are turned out only for about half an hour each day— just long enough for the farmer to clean and bed the stalls with fresh straw.

If you are in the barn during milking time

you'll probably see the milking done by machine. The milking machine is run by electricity or a gasoline engine. The milking machine milks a cow in about 3 minutes.

The milking machine itself looks like a big, covered jug. It has four tubes that connect the big jug to the cow's udders. The cow's udders have been washed and dried before the tubes are attached. Air suction keeps the tubes attached to the udders.

The milking machine is made of stainless steel. Stainless steel is a metal that is easy to clean. It's also possible to regulate temperature through stainless steel. After each milking the machines are taken apart and cleaned.

As each cow is milked the jug on the milking machine fills. Then the milk from the pot is poured into a pail which is marked with the name and number of the cow. Each pail of milk is weighed and the weight is written down in the record for each cow.

After it is weighed, you can see the milk strained and dumped into big milk cans, covered and cooled to await the trip to the dairy. The milk cools in the farmer's milkhouse. The farmer may take the cooled cans

of milk to market or to the railroad station. Sometimes the cans of milk are picked up by a truck from the dairy.

Today most of the farms are using the more modern way of getting their milk to the dairy. This is called bulk pickup. The milk goes from the barn to the farmer's milkhouse. It may be carried in cans or pumped through pipes directly into a cooler tank. Then the dairy truck pulls up to the milkhouse and hooks up a pipe from the

truck to the cooler tank in the milkhouse. Then the cooled milk is pumped right into the truck's tank.

The milk truck has a big, long round body called a tank. It is very much like a big thermos bottle on wheels. The inside is made of stainless steel, and it holds about 4,000 gallons of milk.

The temperature of the milk when it is put into the truck is about 40° F. The tank keeps the milk at this same cold temperature until it is delivered to the dairy.

The tanker carries the milk to the pasteurizing plant. When you visit the dairy plant you may see the milk tankers delivering their loads of milk.

The trucks drive into the garage under the building. The tanker hooks the spout that is on the back of the truck tank onto a pipe leading into the plant. The milk is then

15

pumped out of the truck tank, through the pipe, up to the holding tanks on the pasteurizing floor.

On the top of the tanker you can see an opening that looks like a manhole cover. This cover is vacuum tight, which means that the cover is sucked on from the inside by lack of air in the tank.

This hole is used when the tank is washed out. A man climbs right down through the hole into the tank. He washes and scrubs the inside thoroughly. Then the tank is ready for its next trip out to collect the farmer's milk.

The milk that is pumped up to the holding tank on the pasteurizing floor is called raw milk. It will be called raw milk until it has been pasteurized. Pasteurizing is the

way of killing the harmful germs in milk, if any are present, with carefully controlled heat.

You'll hear the noise on the pasteurizing floor before you even get to it. Once you get to the big room you'll see huge tanks and machines down both sides of the room. A network of pipes connects the machines and tanks of milk.

You can see that all the tanks, pipes, and machines are made of stainless steel. Every night the machines and pipes are taken apart and washed and sterilized. Sterilization is a way of being sure that all machinery parts that touch the milk are clean and safe. The inside of the tanks are also washed and sterilized. The floors are scrubbed and everything is kept clean. The workers all wear white jackets and pants. Everything is as clean and white as milk.

The men start the milk on its way through the many steps of pasteurizing and bottling twice a day. You can't see the milk because it's inside the tanks, pipes and machines. But you sure can hear the machines running.

The milk is kept in storage tanks where

it is kept cool until it is needed. These storage tanks are at the far end of the room. They are big round tanks with pipes on one side for the milk to run into the tank, and pipes on the other side for milk to run out of it.

Each tank of milk is checked by a man called the tester. The tester checks a sample of milk to be sure that it is safe and clean and rich enough. The tester must give a release slip before the milk in a tank may be used.

The milk from the storage or holding tank is piped to a machine called the clarifier. The clarifier has a small body about the size of a wastepaper basket, but it has a cover

that comes to a point on top. Inside the clarifier are little cold pieces of metal that spin very fast. These spinning disks mix up the milk. If by any chance there is anything that shouldn't be in the milk it drops to the bottom of the machine. This is one of the many safeguards dairies use to protect the milk, even though it has been guarded for cleanliness every step of the way.

From the clarifier the milk runs through the pipes and machines. If too much milk went through the machines, it would over-flow or back up. If too little milk went through the pipes, air would get into the machines. Air in the pipes would make the milk foamy. The balance tank keeps just the right amount of milk flowing into the pipes and machines.

The milk then goes through a machine called a regenerator. The regenerator is the tall thin machine that you can see. It is divided into two parts, one side is hot and one side is cold. The milk from the balance tank runs through the pipes into the side that is hot. This starts heating the milk and begins the pasteurization.

After the milk leaves the regenerator it flows through the pipes into the heater. The milk gets hotter and hotter. When it leaves the heater it runs through the pipes to the homogenizer. The homogenizer mixes the cream into the milk.

The rich creamy part of milk is called butter fat. In skim milk all the butter fat or cream is taken out of the milk. In regular milk the cream rises to the top of the milk. In homogenized milk the cream is mixed right into the milk.

The homogenizer breaks the butter fat into tiny pieces so small that you couldn't even see them. It mixes and shakes the milk until the cream is so well mixed into the milk that it will never separate from it again.

After the milk leaves the homogenizer it travels very quickly through a large pipe called the holding tube. The holding tube is right next to the regenerator. When the milk gets to the end of the holding tube it is sent through the other side of the regenerator. This is the cold side and the milk is cooled.

In front of this holding tube and the regenerator you'll see a big board about the size of your blackboard in school. This board is the control board for the pasteurizing. It has many dials and many huge thermometers. These thermometers show the men how hot the milk is in the holding tube and how long it stays hot. If the needle on the dials goes below a certain temperature the milk is sent back to the balance tank. When this happens the milk gets as far as the holding tube where a valve blocks its flow. A valve is like a door that opens and closes in the pipes. When the milk is being returned for more heating, the valve of the holding tube stays closed while another valve opens. This lets the milk flow into pipes which lead back into the balance tank. There the milk must start all over again.

Milk that has been heated just right flows through the other valve into the holding tube and then into the cold part of the regenerator. Then the cooled milk is piped into the holding tank which supplies milk for the bottling machine. When it's time to bottle the milk it is run through pipes from the storage tank down to the bottling machine on the floor below.

When you go downstairs to the bottling floor you'll be in another huge room with lots of machines. The conveyor belts that run between and connect the machines look like a spider web when you look at them from above. But when you see them up close you'll see that they are small moving tracks that carry things to and from the machines.

All the machines are busy. You hear the noise of the machines and the clang of the many bottles. The motors on all the machines are going full blast and it seems that every bottle is moving. There are bottles being washed, bottles being filled, bottles being packed, and bottles always on the move.

When the empty bottles are brought back to the plant they are put through the bottle washer. The bottle fits into a slot on a revolv-

ing belt. This moving belt circles through the huge shiny machine called the bottle washer. As each bottle enters the machine it is sprayed with a special kind of water. An arm with a brush plunges into each bottle and scrubs it out. Next you'll see the bottles pass under scalding water where they are

sterilized, then dried and cooled. The moving track called the bottle feeder takes the sparkling clean bottles right over to the next machine. As they pass in parade, the bottles are carefully inspected to make sure that only perfect ones are filled with milk.

The milk has come through the pipes from

the pasteurizing floor into a machine called the bottle filler. This machine has a large tank which holds the milk. At the bottom of the tank are many small spouts the size of the milk-bottle top.

The bottle feeder moves the bottles into place under the bottle filler. As each bottle top fits under a spout, milk flows into it. The machine is regulated to give out just a quart of milk, so that the bottles never overflow.

Another job of the bottle filler is to cap and seal the bottles. You can watch the bottles fill with milk. Then as they keep going around the machine you'll see a cap drop into place. Then if you look quickly you'll see an arm shoot down on top of the bottle and clamp on the cap.

The filled and capped bottles of milk are carried along on the moving track right out

of the other side of the machine. The bottle has made a complete circle. You can see the full bottles and the empty ones pass each other as the full bottles are leaving the machine and the empty ones are going into the machine.

The filled bottles move along the track and around to the next machine where the bottles are lined up for packing in clean cases. This is done by stopping the bottles—three at a time—at the end of the track. The first three bottles move aside to make room for the next three, and so it goes—just like a parade of bottles.

When there are three rows of three bottles, you will see a rack come down over the nine bottles and pick them up. The rack sets them into a case that slides into position under the bottles.

Then the case of milk bottles travels on the conveyor belt out to the loading room. The temperature in this room is only a little above freezing. Here milk quickly cools and stays cool until it is time to load the trucks.

The cooled delivery trucks back right up to the loading-room platform. Then the cases of cold milk are loaded onto the trucks and are ready for delivery to you—at your home or your grocery store.

The milkman delivers the milk all over your town. He comes to your house and puts the milk right on your doorstep. He goes to the stores, restaurants and school cafeterias.

There are many other kinds of milk—milk that has different vitamins added, milk that has more cream than other milk, and milk that has different flavors added.

Probably one of your favorite kinds of milk is chocolate milk. When you visit the dairy plant you can see over in one corner of the pasteurizing room a big tank. Chocolate milk is mixed in this tank. Chocolate syrup is put into homogenized milk. It is

stirred until it is smooth and creamy. Then it too goes through the same bottling process as the homogenized milk.

Another kind of milk is skim milk, milk without any cream in it. It is not as yellowish in color as homogenized milk, nor is it so rich in cream. Skim milk is used for cooking sometimes and sometimes for baby-formulas. It's also used in many diets that doctors order. The milk is separated from the cream in a machine called the separator. The milk goes through this machine after it has left the clarifier and before it goes to a balance tank.

Buttermilk is made from skim milk and special bacteria. These bacteria are so small that you can't see them. They are called a culture. The dairy buys this special culture from a chemical laboratory. It comes in a tiny bottle. But this tiny bottle holds enough bacteria for many thousands of quarts of buttermilk.

A little tiny bit of the culture is put into a bottle of sterile skim milk. Then the bottle is put into a warm storage room the day before it is to be used. The bottle of milk sits and waits for the culture to grow in the storage—or aging—room. The bacteria multiplies very fast. Soon there is enough bacteria in that one bottle of milk to make buttermilk out of a whole tank of skim milk. The next day the bottle of culture is added to the tank of skim milk. Then the tank of milk is stored until it is buttermilk. Soon it's buttermilk-bottling time. This kind of buttermilk is called cultured buttermilk.

Cottage cheese is made in much this same way. Special culture is added to skim milk. The skim milk, after it has thickened, is called curd. The thick part is separated from the whey, which is the liquid part. This dry curd is added to sour cream and mixed with a big stick in a huge tub. At the end of the

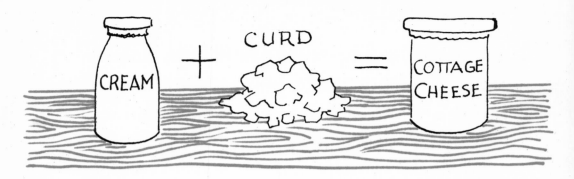

CREAM + CURD = COTTAGE CHEESE

pasteurizing floor you will be able to see a man stirring the cheese in this big tub. When it is thoroughly mixed the cottage cheese is ready for boxing.

The great tubs of cottage cheese are taken down from the pasteurizing floor to the bottling floor. In one corner of the bottling floor is a machine much like the bottling machine used for milk. The cheese is in the top of the machine and is fed into the paper cartons as they pass underneath the opening. Then the cartons are capped and cased, and ready for the store.

Sour cream is made from light cream and a special culture that thickens it. It also is put in the aging room until it is smooth, creamy and just the right flavor.

When you leave the dairy plant you will know that your health is being safeguarded by all the men and machines you have seen. Your milk and milk products have had a long and careful journey from the cow in her stall to you.

WORDS YOU WILL HEAR AT THE DAIRY

Balance tank—machine used to give an even flow of milk.

Bottle feeder—moving track that takes the bottles in for filling.

Bottle filler—machine that fills the bottles with milk.

Bottle washer—machine that washes the empty bottles.

Clarifier—machine that gets rid of dirt in the milk.

Feed bunk—holds cows' food, also called a manger.

Homogenizer—machine that mixes the cream into the milk.

Pasteurizing—killing any harmful germs in milk by heat.

Pickup tanker—truck that collects milk from farmers

Raw milk—milk before it has been pasteurized.

Regenerator—machine divided into two parts—one for heating and one for cooling the milk.

Separator—machine that separates the cream from the milk.

Stalls—where the cow eats and sleeps in the barn.

Sterilization—killing all living cells.

Storage tank—tank at the dairy where milk is kept cold before used.